What Makes POPCORN

POP

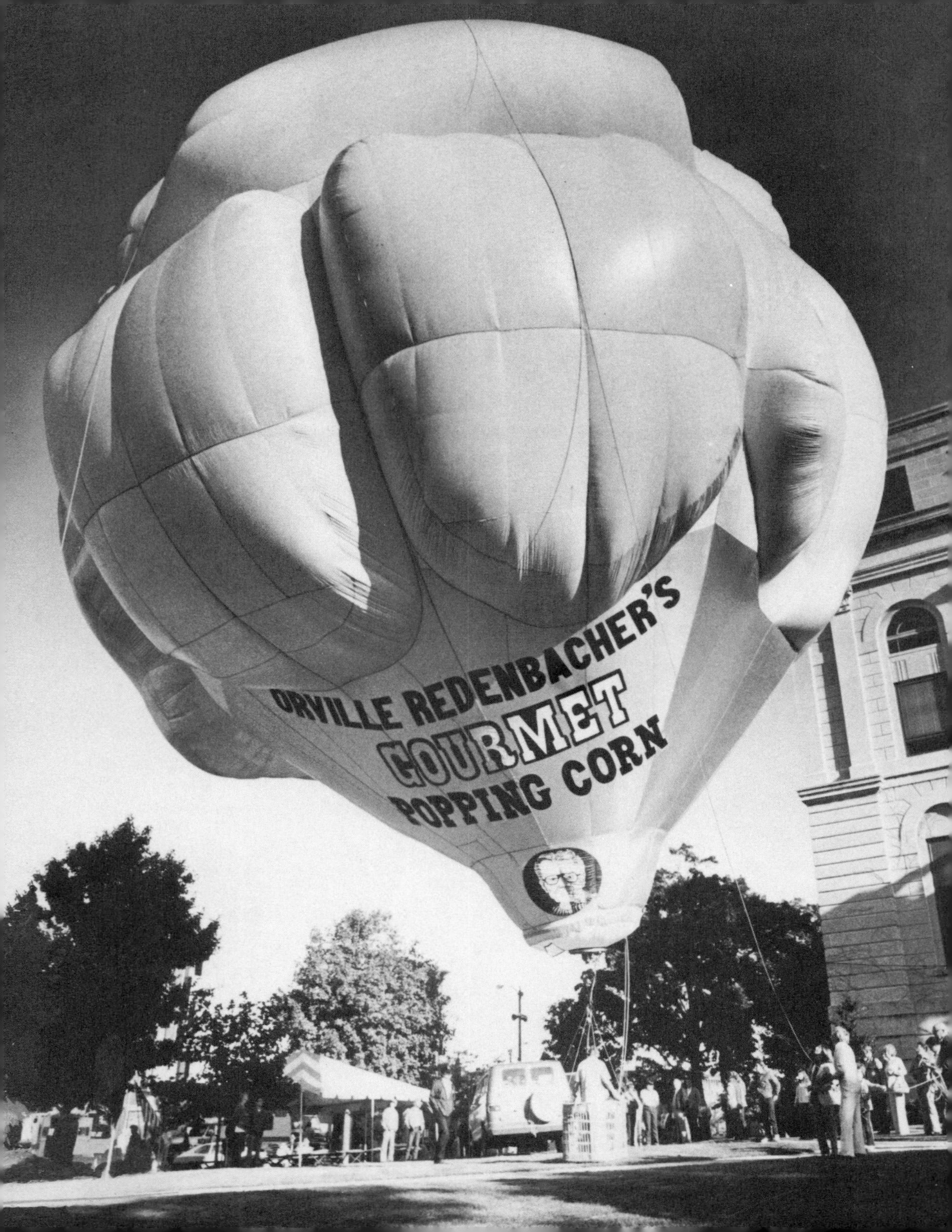
ORVILLE REDENBACHER'S
GOURMET
POPPING CORN

What Makes POPCORN

POP

by DAVE WOODSIDE

Illustrated with old prints, photographs

and drawings by Kay Woon

Atheneum ☐ 1980 ☐ New York

**Library of Congress Cataloging in
Publication Data**

Woodside, Dave.
  What makes popcorn pop?

  SUMMARY: Traces the history of popcorn
describing how to grow and prepare it, its
varied uses, myths surrounding it, and what
makes it pop.
  1. Popcorn—Juvenile literature.
[1. Popcorn] I. Woon, Kay. II. Title.
TX799.W66   641.6'5677   80-12712
ISBN 0-689-30794-2

Text copyright © 1980 by Dave Woodside
Illustrations copyright © 1980 by
  Atheneum Publishers, Inc.
Published simultaneously in Canada by
McClelland & Stewart, Ltd.
Manufactured by R.R. Donnelley & Sons,
  Crawfordsville, Indiana
Designed by M. M. Ahern
First Edition

Picture credits

American Pop Corn Company: 62
Cracker Jack a trademark of Borden, Inc.:
  21
C. Cretors & Company: 16-17, 19, 24-25
Hunt-Wesson Foods/Orville Redenbacher's
  Gourmet Popping Corn: Frontispiece,
  40, 46-49, 51
Lily Division, Owens-Illinois: vii, 9, 14, 27,
  56, 61,
Ross Mehan: 31, 32, 43, 44
Organization of American States: 7, 8,
  11 (right)
University Museum, University of
  Pennsylvania: 11 (left)

Contents

To Kathy.
You showed me how.

What Makes POPCORN

POP

pop.corn (pop′corn′), *n.* 1. any of several varieties
of corn whose kernels burst open and puff out
when subjected to dry heat.
2. popped corn [short for *popped corn.*
See POP[1], -ED[2], CORN[1]]

Popcorn: America's Favorite Mystery Food

It was 1492, and Christopher Columbus was lost.

The Queen of Spain thought he was on his way to India.

The people who lent him money thought he was on his way to India.

Even his crew thought he was on his way to India.

Instead, he stumbled onto a strange Atlantic island a half a world away. And accidentally discovered two of the most explosive forces ever found by a European: America and popcorn.

You know plenty about America.

But what do you know about popcorn?

Do you know, for instance, that popcorn is a special corn?

Do you know what makes it different from other corn? Or where it comes from? Or even what makes it pop?

Don't feel bad.

Even though Americans munch through seven and a quarter BILLION quarts of it a year, most of them know less about popcorn than Columbus knew about finding India.

3

Why Take Popcorn Seriously?

Even if you hate puppies and never laugh, you probably like popcorn. Popcorn is eaten at movies, carnivals, fairs, circuses, amusement parks, ball games—almost anywhere people get together to have a good time. And because it's such a good time snack, no one takes it seriously. Who wants to spoil a good time by studying it, or even reading about it?

Well listen. We could learn a lot from popcorn. For one thing, we could learn something about ancient history.

Popcorn originated in Mexico. Yet is some parts of China, Sumatra and India, people have grown popcorn since before Columbus discovered America.

How did it get all the way to China? When? By what route? Did popcorn somehow float across the Pacific Ocean by itself? Did the Chinese come to America long, long ago and take popcorn back with them? Or did the Indians of America discover the rest of the world before the world discovered them?

No one knows the answers. Yet. But popcorn raised these questions, so maybe popcorn will help answer them, too.

While it's fun to study history, there is a more important reason for studying popcorn. And that reason is its ability to survive. Popcorn can grow in parts of the world other corns can't. When scientists find the secret of the popcorn plant's hardiness, they might be able to transfer it to other types of corn plants. Then other corns could grow in parts of the world they can't grow now and

help solve the world's hunger problem.

And that's why we take popcorn seriously.

The Bible Had Corn All Wrong

When the Bible talks about corn, it's not really talking about corn. Because corn never existed in Biblical countries during the time the Bible was written. The "corn" stored in the pyramids of Egypt during the Seven Years of Plenty was probably barley.

In 1436, fifty-six years before Columbus discovered the New World and popcorn, the English Corn Laws were passed. That "corn" was wheat.

In Scotland and Ireland, "corn" was oats.

Why all the confusion?

In the old days, the most common grain of any particular area was always called "corn." When maize (the Indian word for our corn) was discovered, it was called "corn" because it was the most common grain in America.

The name stuck.

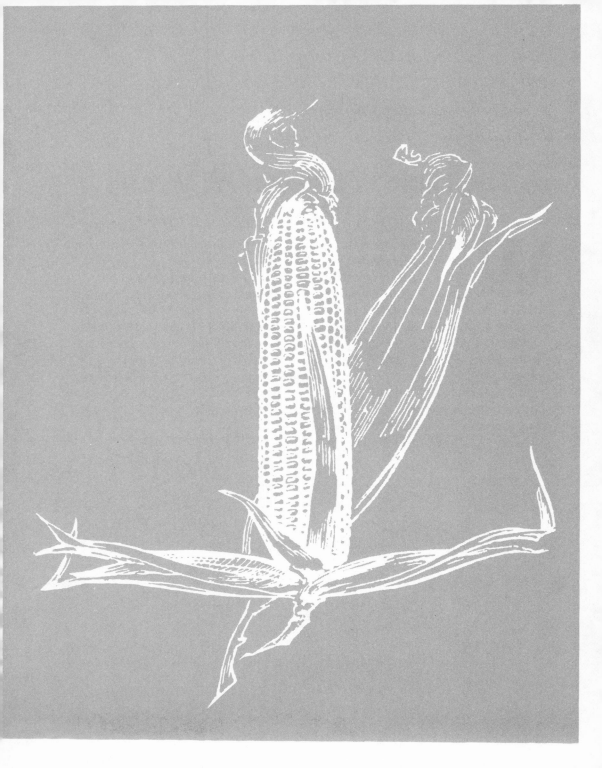

The Thousand Year Old Popcorn That Still Pops

I n Peru, thousand-year-old tombs holding the bodies of Incan leaders also held gold, jewels—and popcorn kernels. The popcorn was probably stored in the tombs so the dead men would have a little something to snack on during their long stay. The dead men weren't disappointed. Because even after a thousand years, the popcorn still popped. The cool dry environment that's perfect for preserving bodies was also perfect for preserving popcorn.

Corn in a gourd bowl from a pre-Incan tomb.

Maize, the "corn" of the New World

In Chile, some deserts haven't had rain for hundreds of years. Winds shifting these desert sands have uncovered popped kernels many centuries old, but still looking fresh and white.

In the Bat Caves of New Mexico, Indians left a six-foot-deep layer of garbage on the floor over the course of three thousand years. Anthropologists like garbage. They dig through it to find things that tell them about the people who lived a long time ago. In the Bat Cave garbage, they found 5,600-year-old popcorn ears, the oldest ever found.

Popcorn has been in the Americas much longer than man. Scientists think it originated in Mexico over eighty thousand years ago. They think it was the first corn, the grand-daddy of all others. And they think it was the first corn eaten by Indians.

Now, without actually being there, how could scientists know that?

Scientists have found much more popcorn lying around pre-historic Indian ruins than other types of corn.

The thousand-year-old popcorn that still pops was uncovered in an Incan tomb similar to this one.

This could be the archaeologist who discovered an ear of popcorn in New Mexico's Bat Cave identified by radio-carbon tests to be 5,600 years old. This discovery upset the theory that corn originated in Peru, where the oldest corn that has been found dates back only to about 1000 B.C. What's more, a 1,000-year-old popped kernel of popcorn was found in a dry cave in southwestern Utah. It was stale.

The corn had kernels as hard as glass, and it's a safe bet that even primitive Indians did not like to chew glass. So the Indians probably ignored corn until one of them accidentally dropped a few glass-hard kernels into the fire. The heat of the fire caused the kernels to pop and fly out of the fire. The startled cook, wary at first, probably swallowed his fear, picked up the popcorn, sniffed it, licked it, and ate it.

Man has been eating popcorn ever since.

Indians—The World's Greatest Popcorn Experts

Indians were popcorn fanatics.

By the time Columbus discovered America, they were growing over seven hundred types of popcorn. They were building fancy poppers, making ceremonial popcorn headdresses and necklaces, wearing popcorn in their hair, making popcorn beer, even selling it. The Indians of San Salvador greeted Columbus and his crew by trying to sell them popcorn corsages.

Popcorn meant so much to the Zapotecs of Mexico, in fact, they painted pictures of popcorn on the sides of funeral urns.

Because many native American civilizations depended on popcorn, they were afraid of losing it. As insurance, the Aztecs would honor Tlaloc,

In Incan days, it was customary to bury pottery, utensils, jewelry, food and fabric with the dead. Notice the corn carved into the side of the vase.

their God of Maize, Rain and Fertility, by decorating statues of him with strands of popcorn. A happy Tlaloc would bring good crops and good fishing for the year.

It must have worked.

In some remote Mexican villages, popcorn is still used to decorate statues of the Virgin Mary.

A stone relief carving of the Maya corn god from Guatamala.

Popcorn At The First Thanksgiving Feast

The Iroquois Indians were invited to the first three-day Thanksgiving feast. When they got there, the Indians saw that the colonists didn't really have much of a feast. So they went into the woods and killed deer and gathered enough fruit and nuts to feed everyone.

One Indian, the chief's brother, Quadequina, brought back a deerskin bag full of popcorn as his dinner gift. In this way, he helped establish the tradition of bringing popcorn as a token of good will during peace negotiations.

The History Of Popcorn Popping

The Indian who discovered the pop in popcorn by accidentally dropping it into the fire discovered the simplest way to cook it. All he needed was heat and popcorn.

But the Indians weren't dumb. They could see that when they tossed popcorn into the fire, they burned more than they ate. So the Indians brought up sand from the shore of a river or lake and heated it in the fire. When the sand was scorching hot, they spread it in front of the fire and stirred in the popcorn until it popped.

Other Indians were even more ingenious. They invented poppers that used the same basic elements as our poppers today: heat, oil and a pan of some sort. Some pans were merely hollowed out soapstones. Some, like the fifteen-hundred-year-old poppers found on the north coast of Peru, were made of clay and metal and had a lid with a hole in the top to let steam escape. These ancient poppers are very similar to the "ollas" the Papago Indians of Arizona and Mexico use to pop popcorn today. Ollas, though, are a little larger—sometimes eight feet across.

In the middle of the seventeenth century, a Spaniard named Felix de Azara explored Paraguay. He found

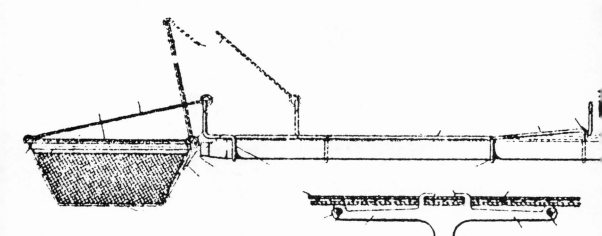

the Indians there cooking a unique type of popcorn. When the Indians pulled the silk strands off the ear, the kernels peeled off, too, remaining attached to the silk. When the kernels were dipped in boiling fat or oil, they popped without flying off the ends of the silk. According to Azara, "There results a superb bouquet fit to adorn a lady's hair at night without anyone knowing what it was. I have often eaten these burst grains and found them very good." (Azara must have been a very dedicated explorer to eat ornaments out of women's hair.)

With another type of popcorn, the Indians spread oil on the ear and lay it near the fire. The kernels popped, but stayed attached to the ear. The Indians would then bite into the ear the way you'd bite into corn-on-the-cob.

As recently as the early 1900s, the Winnebago Indians of the Great Lakes popped popcorn by poking a sharp stick through the cob and holding it near the flames. The Winnebagos were very careful with their popcorn supply. To make sure that no one would take more than his or her fair share, they enforced a very strict rule: No person could pop an ear longer than the distance between his or her ribs.

With their budding Yankee know-how, the American colonists brought out their crude tools and set to work hammering out their own style of

14

popcorn poppers. They flattened a sheet of iron and punched holes in it. Then, with the popcorn on the iron, they laid it on the fire. As the iron heated up, the kernels popped off into their hands.

But scrambling around to catch the flying kernels was hard work and it certainly wasn't very dignified. So they bent the iron sheets into cylinders, put the popcorn in the cylinders, and turned them on axles in front of a hot fire. Then none of the kernels could escape.

We've come a long way. Our popcorn poppers have changed quite a bit. But almost all of them still use the same elements the Indians used over a thousand years ago: heat, oil and a pan.

Charlie Cretors And The First Automatic Popcorn Popper

The year was 1885, and Charlie Cretors made peanut roasters.

One day, people passing Charlie Cretor's place in Chicago were amazed to see a small machine that chugged and popped and chugged and popped. It was steam-powered, and it was popping popcorn. This was new. Up to that time, popcorn had always been popped in a wire basket over an open flame, even by street-corner vendors. Char-lie Cretors had made the first popcorn popping machine.

Some of the people passing his place that day were salesmen on the way to the railroad station for trips across the country. These salesmen told storekeepers they met in their travels about the amazing "popcorn

The first popcorn machines stood outside stores to attract people walking by.

15

popping machine" they'd seen in front of Charlie Cretor's.

"Not bad", thought some of the storekeepers. If we could just get our hands on that automatic popcorn popping machine, our popcorn would be easier and cleaner to pop.

So they asked the salesmen to have Charlie make them a popcorn popping machine. And in a short time, Charlie's main business was making popcorn poppers.

At first, almost all the poppers were made to sit in front of stores to attract attention. But the popcorn vendors wanted to be close to the crowds, especially the crowds that stood in front of movie theaters. So Charlie made poppers that could be pushed on foot, pulled by horse, and mounted on trucks.

Charlie Cretors was very successful. Even today, much of the popcorn you buy at movies and fairs is popped in poppers made by Charlie Cretor's family.

Charlie Cretors had another important role in popcorn history. He popularized the old Indian trick of popping popcorn in oil.

Popcorn Makes The Big Time

Times were good for America in the late 1890s.

More people had more money to spend. And one of the things they spent it on was popcorn. While the ancient Indians needed popcorn for survival, the Gay Nineties American needed popcorn for a good time. They couldn't get enough of it. Street vendors followed the crowds around, pushing steam or gas-powered poppers through fairs and parks and expositions. Whenever someone wanted popcorn, someone else was there to sell it, hot and covered with lard. Popcorn was on its way to becoming a big business.

During the depression in the 1930s, popcorn at five cents or ten cents a bag was one of the few luxuries down-and-out families could afford. While other businesses failed, the popcorn business thrived. An Oklahoma banker, who went broke when his bank failed, bought a popcorn machine and started business in a small store near a theater. In a

18

Popcorn at five cents a bag was a good deal.

couple of years, his popcorn business made enough money to buy back three of the farms he'd lost.

Later, during World War II, sugar was sent overseas for U.S. troops. So there wasn't much sugar left in the States to make candy. The country's sweet tooth ached. America's treat freaks, not finding their sweets, ate three times as much popcorn as usual. At the same time, the United States government was also sending popcorn overseas. A popcorn shortage developed. Thousands of popcorn vending machines closed down. Theater profits slumped. A popcorn black market was even organized, where popcorn was bought and sold illegally.

America was definitely on a popcorn binge. It was the perfect American snack. It was good. It was cheap. And it made the popcorn vendor a lot of money. It only cost the vendor two cents for the popcorn he sold for ten cents. If theater owners sold a thousand bags a day, as many claimed, they made as much as eighty dollars a day. A typical small movie house made four hundred to one thousand dollars a week on popcorn alone.

The only time that popcorn wasn't a good business was in the early 1950s, when the television first became popular. The more people watched television, the less they went to theaters. Popcorn sales dropped as theater attendance dropped. It wasn't until advertising taught the public to eat popcorn at home that popcorn became a healthy business again.

Today, the average American eats thirty-three quarts of popcorn a year.

"That's a Cracker Jack®"

For two German Brothers, 1893 was a very important year. Twenty years earlier, they'd been selling popcorn on a Chicago streetcorner. Now they were introducing a hard and sticky popcorn, peanut and molasses candy to the more than twenty-one million visitors at the Chicago World Columbian Exposition. The brothers hoped it would be liked.

It was.

It was Cracker Jack®.

Actually, at the Exposition, it wasn't

Can you name the boy and his dog?

Cracker Jack® yet. Cracker Jack® didn't get its name until a few years later. The brothers had just discovered how to keep the molasses coated popcorn from sticking together during its shipping in wooden tubs. A salesman, upon tasting it, said "That's a cracker jack." The brothers heard the salesman and immediately renamed the candy "Cracker Jack®." And a little while later, when a customer wrote, "The more you eat, the more you want," the brothers adopted that phrase as the slogan you still see on the box.

In the early 1900s, people rummaging through their boxes of Cracker Jack® began finding coupons that could be sent in for prizes. People liked the coupons so they bought more Cracker Jack®. They bought so much more, the company decided to put the actual prizes in the package. And except for the time the United States was at war with Japan, where the prizes are made, there's been a prize in every box ever since. After the war, when the Japanese began making the prizes again, over twenty million were given away each month. Today, the Cracker Jack® company appoints a prize committee whose only job is to pick Cracker Jack® prizes.

Through the years, the Cracker Jack® company has tried selling different kinds of popcorn candies like Prize Chums, Cracker Jack® Brittle, Fruit Popcorn, Chocolate Covered Cracker Jack®, even French Fried Popcorn. But Cracker Jack® has always been the favorite, and billions of boxes have been sold in the United States and fifty-three countries. In fact, the Cracker Jack® company is the largest buyer of popcorn in the world.

A trivia question:

Everybody has seen a Cracker Jack® box and everybody has seen the sailor boy and his dog, on the box since 1919.

Can you name them?

ANSWER: Jack and Bingo

"To Make Money, Buy A Good Popcorn Machine and Build a Movie Theater Around It."

Theater owners used to hate popcorn.

"It's too noisy," they said. "Too messy."

But moviegoers loved it. So the vendors who sold popcorn to the moviegoers standing in lines outside cleaned up profits while the theater owners cleaned up spilled popcorn.

It didn't seem fair.

Some theaters made their customers leave their popcorn at the door. Others called the police to chase the popcorn vendors off the street. But it didn't help. The vendors made too much money to give up. So they moved their popcorn business into nearby stores. The moviegoers just stopped at the stores before they stopped at the theaters.

The theaters finally wised up. If they had to clean up the popcorn anyway, they might as well make some money on it. And they did. Right from the beginning, some theaters made more money from popcorn than they made from movies. A Texan who bought a

SECRET LOVES

At first, most popcorn machines were outside the theaters.

theater in the 1930s from a man who refused to sell popcorn told this story:

"I just took this theater over on a mortgage because the man running it went broke. But the old fellow who used to have a popcorn machine outside bought a house, a store, and a farm." The Texan didn't make the same mistake. He sold popcorn.

Popcorn was so popular that bad popcorn hurt theater business more than bad movies. When business was slow, many theaters lowered the price of their tickets so more people would come to the theater and buy popcorn. Theaters lost money on the movies, but made it all back on popcorn sales.

The moviegoers did have one major gripe against popcorn, although it wasn't really popcorn's fault. The paper bags the popcorn was served in were noisy. One hun-dred people reaching into paper bags during a particularly romantic scene could ruin the romance for good.

This was a serious matter. One theater owner was so afraid the noise would hurt his popcorn sales that he replaced the paper bags with silent plastic bags. Within days, four times as many people were buying his popcorn. But not only because the bags were silent. The clear plastic had a yellow tint, which made his popcorn look drenched in butter. A lot of people bought his popcorn because they thought it had more butter on it.

For some reason, the plastic bags never caught on. But the crackle problem was solved by serving pop-corn in paper buckets. The buckets are quiet in another way, too.

They can't be blown up and popped.

The noise problem was solved by serving popcorn in paper buckets.

26

The Trick to Selling Popcorn at the Movies

One theater owner made a mistake. She moved her popcorn machine where her customers couldn't see it. People stopped buying her popcorn, and she couldn't figure out why. It was the same popcorn, and she hadn't raised the price. But as soon as she moved the machine back to where her customers could see it, sales jumped back up again.

The Popcorn Institute, a group of popcorn businesses that banded together to help each other, tells theater owners how to avoid this kind of mistake. Here are some of their ideas for how theater owners can sell more popcorn.

- Tickets should be taken at the door closest to the popcorn machines, so moviegoers have to walk past the popper to get to the movie.
- Make sure you have intermissions. They put people into the lobby, near the poppers. They're more likely to buy when it's in front of their noses.

- The poppers should be flashy, with lots of lights and colors. One theater owner said that when the popcorn popper lights go out, sales fall ten percent. If popcorn is spotlighted, sales jump twenty percent.
- Posters and banners can boost sales from ten percent to twenty percent.
- Movement attracts people. One moving display can increase sales as much as five percent.
- Show ads between movies. When you see the larger-than-life box of popcorn on the screen, something clicks in your head and you start craving popcorn.
- Pop your popcorn in artificially colored oil. It makes the popcorn look like it has butter on it. Popcorn popped in peanut and coconut oil tastes better than popcorn popped in corn oil.
- Show comedies and action movies. They sell more popcorn than dramas and romances. Abbott and Costello, a comedy team in the '40s and '50s, seemed to sell the most popcorn.

28

● Use "anhydrous" butter—butter with the curds and whey removed. It melts in your mouth, and is less greasy looking.

How to Pop the Best Popcorn at Home

Proper Popping Paraphernalia

Stainless steel or lightweight aluminum skillet or pan, with lid loose enough to allow steam to escape.

Enough popcorn to cover the bottom of the pan one kernel deep.

Vegetable oil. (Don't use butter. When the pan is hot enough to pop popcorn, butter will burn)

Directions:

1. Measure oil into pan. Use one measure of oil for every three measures of popcorn.
2. Place pan on medium-high to high heat
3. Drop in one or two kernels
4. When the kernel pops, or spins in the oil, add the rest of the popcorn, cover, and shake the pan.
5. When the popping slows, take the pan off the heat. The remaining heat will pop the rest of the corn.

The secret to perfect popping lies in the amount of oil you use. Since oil spreads the heat evenly around each kernel, make sure the kernels are at least one-third covered with it. If you don't use enough oil, only the first kernels will pop properly. The rest will pop smaller or burn. If you use too much oil, the popcorn will get soaked and taste greasy. One measure of oil for every three measures of popcorn kernels seems to work best. (I once knew a very old hunter who popped perfect popcorn in an old black skillet without any oil. I tried it three times and I burned it three times.)

Don't add salt to the oil. It makes the popcorn tough. Add the salt after the popcorn has popped.

Heat the pan over medium-high to high heat. Too much or too little heat will make the popcorn pop smaller, if it pops at all. The best popping temperature is between 400°F and 460°F. Oil burns at 500°F, so if the oil starts to smoke you know it's too hot.

Toss a kernel or two in the pan as the oil heats. If you aren't a patient person, the minute or so you have to wait for those test kernels to pop will drag on and on and on. But if you don't wait for the test kernels, your popcorn will actually take longer to pop and will pop small and tough and be a general disappointment. So wait. When the test kernels pop, pour the rest of the popcorn into the pan one kernel deep. (One ounce of raw popcorn kernels will pop into one quart of popped popcorn.)

Shake the pan to make sure the oil coats each kernel. Between sixty and ninety seconds after you pour in the popcorn it should be popping furiously, like a machine gun. The faster it pops, the better. In about a minute, the popping will begin to slow down. When it does, take the pan off the heat. The heat remaining in the pan will pop the rest of the kernels for you.

There's one more thing you should know.

The lid to the pan should fit loosely enough to allow the steam to escape. If you don't let the steam escape, it collects on the inside of the lid and then rolls back onto the popcorn to make it tough.

If you follow these directions, and you've been careful to keep your popcorn stored in an airtight con-

The lid should fit loosely enough to allow steam to escape.

tainer, you should get perfect popcorn every time.

Sometime, you should pop your popcorn the old way, with a fireplace popcorn popper. I bought mine at a store that sells fireplace supplies. It's a shallow metal box on the end of a long handle. Just pour in the oil and popcorn, and shake it over a fire. The popcorn seems to pop faster, louder, and somehow taste about seven and a half times better.

Popcorn popped in a fireplace popper tastes about seven and a half times better.

Popping Popcorn the Electric Way

In 1978, Americans popped over five billion quarts of popcorn at home, much of it in electric popcorn poppers. The first home electric poppers came out around 1925, and by the early 1930s junior high school students were building them in shop classes for as little as a dollar apiece.

Electric poppers aren't very complicated and usually do a pretty good job. Basically, they're just a heating element with a container to hold the oil and popcorn. Some get fancy and cost a lot of money, but you're mostly paying for the looks.

Watch out for the ones that add butter while the corn is actually popping. The butter will make the popcorn tough. If you want buttered popcorn, melt the butter yourself and add it to the popcorn after it's popped.

There is one electric popper, though, that's different. Instead of popping the kernels in oil, it blasts the popcorn with very hot air. Without oil the bowl of popcorn is cheaper and has fewer calories. There's only one hitch. Without oil, salt won't stick to the popcorn. And to popcorn lovers, popcorn without salt is like a dog without hair.

In 1945, at a Raytheon plant near Boston, a fellow named Percy Spencer made an amazing discovery. When he put popcorn in a field of microwave energy, it popped. This inspired him to heat other foods with microwave energy. They cooked, too. An oven was made, and microwave cooking was born.

A friend of mine once showed me a neat trick with her microwave oven. She put a little oil and some popcorn kernels in a paper bag, placed the bag in the microwave, set it on high, and in a few minutes she had a bag of popped popcorn.

Real magic.

But her best trick was putting the flames out, because the paper bag caught fire. She had closed off the paper bag with a metal tie that heated to a red glow and ignited the paper.

So play it safe. If you're going to pop popcorn in a microwave oven, follow the manufacturer's directions. You'll get near-perfect, flame-free popcorn.

Popcorn at the Campsite

It's easy to pop popcorn when you're camping if you take a few tips from the Indians. The simplest way is to toss a handful of kernels next to a burning log. Some will pop out at you, but most won't. They'll pop right back into the fire. You'll burn about three-fourths of your popcorn, but if you don't have anything to pop your popcorn in, it's better than nothing.

For a little more luck, heat sand in a fire. When the sand is very hot, clear a space next to the fire and spread the hot sand in the space. Then stir the popcorn into the sand. The heat from the fire and sand together should pop it.

Or try another old Indian trick. Place flat stones next to a very hot fire. (WATCH OUT: VERY SMOOTH, ROUNDED STONES FORMED IN RIVER BEDS CAN EXPLODE WHEN PLACED IN A FIRE. MAKE SURE THAT THE STONES ARE FLAT AND DO NOT COME FROM A RIVER BED OR OLD STREAM BED) After your stones heat up, set the kernels on the stones. And hope the popcorn will pop out of the fire and not into it.

If you have a thick-bottomed pan with a lid, set it on the hot coals and cook the popcorn the same way you would at home. Or use a fireplace popcorn popper. Or pop the popcorn that comes in an aluminum pan with a handle.

You might not get the same light and tender popcorn when you're camping as you would popping it at home, but even tough popcorn can make a cool evening a little warmer.

What Makes Popcorn Pop?

There's a lot of hop in the pop.

A whole lot.

If you don't put a lid on your pan, some kernels will pop up to three feet into the air. That's higher than most of you can jump. (As far as I know, though, popcorn is the only vegetable that can outjump you)

The Indians had no idea why popcorn popped, but that didn't stop them from making some guesses.

was finally too hot, he'd blow his top. The popcorn exploded, and the tiny demon disappeared with the steam.

Scientists have found no demon. Yet. But they do think they've found the secret of what makes popcorn pop. And that secret is the water inside the kernel. No water, no pop. So to know why popcorn pops, you need to know what happens to water when it's heated.

Water, like everything, is made up of millions of tiny particles called molecules. They move close together when they're cold and move farther apart when they're hot. As the water gets hotter, the molecules move farther and farther apart, turning to steam, taking up more room.

The water in the popcorn kernel is stored in a tiny glob of soft starch in the middle of the kernel. As the kernel heats up, the water in the glob of soft starch heats up, takes up more room, and builds up pressure. The hard, toenail-like starch surrounding the soft glob resists the pressure of the expanding water. When the kernel gets hot enough, the hard starch is no longer strong enough to hold in the expanding water.

The popcorn explodes.

And the soft starch pushes out, turning the popcorn inside out. The steam inside the kernel is released into the air.

Inside each kernel, they thought, there lived a tiny demon. The demon was comfortable and remained quiet and still as long as he wasn't disturbed. And nothing disturbed him, really, except one thing: Heat. When the kernel got hot, the tiny demon got mad. The hotter the kernel, the madder the demon. He'd shake his house, spinning it around. He'd struggle, pushing from inside, puffing out the walls of the kernel. When it

36

What's Wrong With Your Popcorn?

There is such a thing as bad popcorn.

For every cup of unpopped popcorn, you should end up with between thirty and forty cups of popped popcorn. If you don't, something is wrong with either your popcorn or the way you pop it. And since you're reading this book, you know that from now on there can't be anything wrong with the way you pop it.

Right?

Bad popcorn is usually too dry. It'll pop slowly. You won't hear the *rat-tat-tat-tat* pounding against the lid. Some of the kernels will only split and won't turn inside out. Those that do pop will be smaller than normal.

Although it's almost impossible to find store-bought kernels with too much water in them, you can find them in home grown popcorn. They'll probably be moldy. When you try to pop them, they'll stick to the pan. And if they pop at all, they'll have a rough surface and look like a doughball.

Yuk.

The popcorn you buy from the market should contain the right amount of moisture when you buy it—somewhere around thirteen and a-half percent. When you leave it uncovered on a hot day, it could lose up to one percent moisture. Even a one percent moisture loss can affect the quality of your popcorn. In five days, it could lose up to three percent and be virtually unpoppable. That's why it's smart to store your popcorn

TOO MOIST

TOO DRY

JUST RIGHT

in an airtight glass or Tupperware container instead of the plastic bag it normally comes in. Store it in a cool cupboard instead of the refrigerator.

The air inside refrigerators contains very little moisture, so the popcorn will dry out after a while.

How To Put Life Back Into Old Maids

Sometime, long ago, somebody noticed some leftover unpopped kernels gathered close together, rather lonely, in the bottom of a bowl. They were a sad group: some popped, but not enough; some bloated; some small and hard and unchanged from when they were first put into the pan. And somebody, a bitter old man, no doubt, gave them the name "Old Maids."

Old maids are kernels too dried out to have any life left in them. The longer you leave your kernels in an uncovered container, the more old maids you'll have.

But wait. As useless as your old maids seem, you don't have to throw them away. One guy used to grind them up in a coffee grinder and eat them for breakfast with a little milk and sugar.

If you prefer your popcorn to pop, though, it's easy to put the pop back into pooped-out popcorn. Because it's easy to put the moisture back in.

Farmers do it all the time. If their popcorn get's too dry during a hot spell, they just wait for rain to put the moisture back naturally. Some farmers hose down the popcorn while it's being carried by the conveyor belt to the scalper, the machine that cuts the kernels from the cob. Other farmers store the popcorn in small rooms and pass damp air through it.

You can put the life back into your popcorn, too.

Fill a one-quart jar three quarters full of popcorn. Add one tablespoon of water. Cover the jar with an airtight lid and give it a few good shakes every few minutes until the popcorn has absorbed all the water. You can tell the water is absorbed when you can't see any drops at the bottom of the jar. Store the jar in a cool place. In two or three days, test pop a batch of kernels. If you still get a batch of old maids, add a few more drops of water to the jar, shake it, then let it sit for a couple more days. You shouldn't have trouble with old maids after that.

One word of caution:

Don't drown your old maids. If the popcorn is soaked in water, it'll sprout. Or mold. Or get too soft to pop. Dry out the popcorn by letting it sit in an open container.

Stored properly, your popcorn could pop for years and years and years. Even after a thousand years, remember, the popcorn in the Incan tomb didn't turn into old maids.

The Difference Between Popcorn and Corn-on-the-Cob

There are five types of corn: sweet corn, dent corn, flint corn, pod corn and popcorn.

Sweet corn is the tender, yellow, juicy corn we eat at dinner and on picnics and call corn-on-the-cob. Sweet corn is the corn you raise in your backyard vegetable garden. It's called sweet corn because the kernels contain more sugar than the other corns.

Dent corn is also called cow corn or field corn. Cows love it. So almost all dent corn is grown to fatten up livestock. It can look like sweet corn, but you'd never see it on your dinner table. A long time ago, before I knew any better, a few friends and I sneaked into a farmer's field and snatched what we thought was sweet corn. We took it to our campsite and began cooking it. And cooking it. And cooking it. It was tough to begin with and it just got tougher. It was dent corn, terrible stuff. We never did eat it.

Serves us right.

Flint corn is commonly called Indian corn. It has red, black, blue, yellow and white kernels and is mostly used as a decoration because it's too tough and tasteless to eat.

Pod corn is only seen in flower arrangements. It's pretty to look at, but horrible to eat. Each kernel is covered by a separate husk.

Popcorn is the only corn that pops. Some people would like to believe that popcorn is simply dried sweet corn because the kernels look so much alike, but it just isn't so. If you tried to pop sweet corn, all you'd get is scorched sweet corn.

The different kinds of corn.

Flint corn — hanging on wall
Sweet corn — lower right-hand corner
Popcorn — in basket
Pod corn — single ear on barrel
Dent corn — on barrel

41

zea mays everta

The scientific name for popcorn is *zea mays everta*.

It's a very official name that probably tells scientists a lot. The trouble is, most popcorns have very little in common with each other except that they're corn and they pop. So even so official a name can't tell anybody anything about all the different kinds of popcorns.

Popcorn kernels can be almost any color, from off-white to light gold to deep gold to deep maroon to red to black to hundreds of shades in between. Yellow and white are the colors you'll find in stores. Of those, most people think yellow popcorn tastes best and that's why nine bags of yellow are sold for every one bag of white. In the early 1900s, however, it was exactly opposite. Yellow popcorn was twice as expensive as white popcorn because it was so scarce. Eventually, enough yellow popcorn was grown to make it as cheap as the white. And since the yellow pops larger than the white, vendors could sell an extra bag or two of popped popcorn per pound of raw popcorn. So, through the vendors' salesmanship, yellow became more popular.

Unfortunately, no matter what color the kernels are, once they're popped, the popcorn is always white—although the yellow kernels may have a yellowish tinge. That's because popcorn turns inside out when it's popped, and popcorn is always white inside.

Most popcorn comes in two basic shapes when it's popped: snowflake and mushroom. Snowflake pops up big and is shaped like a cumulus cloud. Mushroom pops smaller, but pops into a round ball. Snowflake popcorn is used in theaters and at home because it looks bigger. Mushroom is used in making popcorn candy because it doesn't crumble in the candy factory.

There are thousands of popcorns, and you'll never see ninety-nine percent of them. Some have unusual shapes, like strawberry popcorn. The short, stubby ear is actually shaped like a strawberry and carries deep strawberry-red kernels.

Some are giants. Although most popcorn plants are smaller than regular corn, Dynamite popcorn has stalks six to eight feet tall and ears eight to nine inches long.

The large ear on the left is sweet corn. The stubby ear on the right is strawberry popcorn. The other four ears are different kinds of popcorn.

And some are freaks. Just a few popped kernels of Snopuff popcorn will fill a bowl.

Out of the thousands of popcorns, only about fifty are considered good enough to sell. Some of the most popular ones are Gurney's Golden Hybrid, Dynamite, Strawberry, Calico,

Popcorn comes in two basic shapes when it is popped: Snowflake, left, and mushroom, right.

Rainbow, Japanese Hulless, Burpees's Peppy Popcorn, Creme-puff, White Cloud, Tom Thumb, and the Gourmet variety.

Be careful when you see the word "hulless" in the name. People don't like popcorn hulls because the hulls get caught between teeth. So popcorn growers would like you to think their popcorn won't have any hulls once it's popped.

Don't believe them.

There's no such thing as hulless popcorn. Sometimes there's a little less hull, and sometimes the hull is a little thinner, but the hull is always there. Even though most of it will shatter into a thousand pieces, called bee wings, you'll always find a little hull caught in your teeth.

Thirty Thousand New Types of Popcorn Every Year

Popcorn is the grandaddy of all corns. It evolved from a wild grass that grew thousands of years ago. That grass is gone now, like the dinosaurs. But popcorn took its place and in an evolution that took many many centuries, the other corns were born.

Popcorn grew just fine on its own for most of these years. Then man started growing it and changing it, and now there is no such thing as wild popcorn anymore. Or wild any-kind-of-corn, for that matter. All corn now needs the help of man before it'll grow.

Man changed popcorn by breeding hybrids. A hybrid is made when one kind of popcorn plant is fertilized with the pollen of another kind of popcorn plant. The seeds that are formed have features and traits from both plants and are called hybrid seeds.

You're a hybrid, in a way. You have features from both your mother and father. Pretend your mother has red hair, blue eyes and light skin. Your father has brown hair, brown eyes and dark skin. If you have red hair from your mother and brown eyes and dark skin from your father, you have features from both your parents. You are a hybrid.

Farmers make hybrids because they want to grow better popcorn. The perfect popcorn pops big, tastes good, resists diseases, has high yield and strong stalks. Hybridization has been successful. Now, for example, popcorn pops up twice as large as it did at the turn of the century.

It's not easy to make the perfect popcorn, though, because making hybrids is a gamble. Just as you can't tell what a child will look like by looking at the parents, you're never sure what the hybrid will be like.

The tassel is covered so that the male pollen won't blow away.

The search for the perfect pop-corn hybrid is serious business. So serious, that two men who work for the Orville Redenbacher Popping Corn Company spend over $100,000 to make over thirty thousand hybrids each year.

Making hybrids is so expensive because it's a tedious process that needs to be done by hand. Each corn plant is both a male and a female. The tassel at the top of the stalk is the male part and sheds pollen when it blooms. The female

The female silk is also covered so pollen won't land on it.

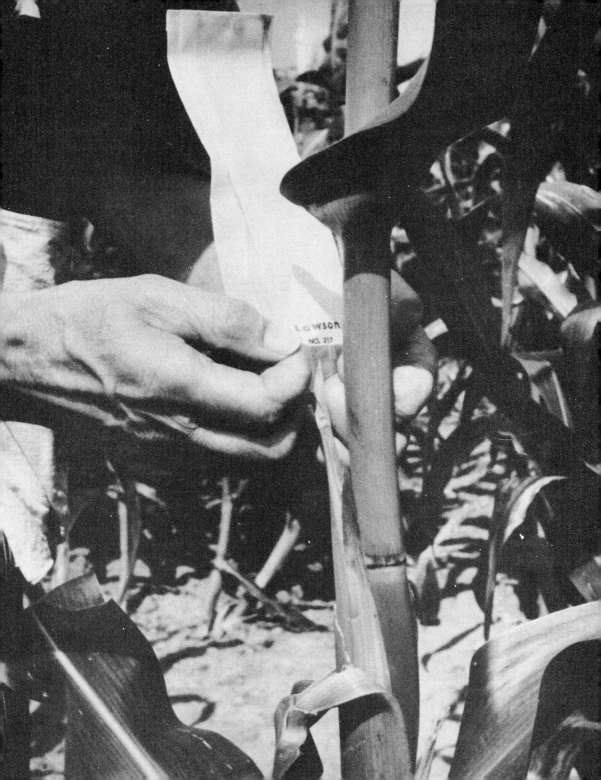

At the right time, the male pollen
is gathered into the sack . . .

. . . and sprinkled onto the silk.

The ears form after pollination.
One kernel will develop for each
pollinated strand of silk.

part is where the silk is attached to the cob. Each strand of silk, when fertilized with one grain of pollen, will produce one kernel. To make the hybrid, the plant breeder shakes the pollen from one type of popcorn plant onto the silk of another type of popcorn plant.

The kernel that is grown is the hybrid seed.

That hybrid seed will grow into a plant. The whole process must be repeated at least ten generations before the hybrid plant will be pure enough to make seeds that faithfully reproduce its traits.

If you want two kinds of popcorn on the same ear, you'd fertilize some of the silk strands with one kind of popcorn pollen and fertilize the other silk strands with another kind. If you were patient enough, and had steady enough hands, you could grow many types of popcorn on one ear by fertilizing each strand of silk with a different popcorn pollen.

Good plant breeders consider themselves lucky if they breed only one significantly improved popcorn in their lives. The Orville Redenbacher breeders, for instance, developed the Gourmet Variety Popcorn in 1965. It's one of the best commercial popcorns ever bred. Yet as of 1979, even with over thirty thousand new hybrids each year, they had not been able to breed a new popcorn that was much better.

No wonder they keep the secret of their popcorn closely guarded.

Growing Four Hundred-Fifty Million Pounds of Popcorn a Year

There're a lot of people in the United States, and most of them eat popcorn.

But that wasn't always true. It wasn't until the 1880s, in fact, that big time farmers began thinking that popcorn might be worth growing. Even then, much wasn't grown until the theaters started demanding it in the 1930s. At that time, most was sold in one hundred and fifty pound bags, or still on the cob in wooden barrels. From nineteen thousand acres in 1912, popcorn production

Orville Redenbacher inspects popcorn ears before they go to the scalper.

was pushed to over one hundred forty-four thousand acres in the late 1970s. Now, over four hundred and fifty million pounds of popcorn are grown every year.

Popcorn is planted in the spring when the danger of frost has passed. Approximately nineteen thousand six hundred seeds per acre are planted. Those seeds weigh between three and eight pounds and produce about two thousand eight hundred pounds of popcorn. It's picked in mid-October when the husks are dry and brown.

In the old days, the farmers snapped the ears off the stalk by hand and shucked the husks off the ears after the popcorn was hauled in from the fields. The ears were stored in wooden corn cribs until the kernels were dry enough to be stripped from the ears and shipped to market.

But now, like most things, popcorn harvesting has become easier and more complicated at the same time. Machines are used, now, which save time and money. The only trouble is that machines can bruise popcorn, affecting its poppability. The advantages of the machines are great, however, so popcorn is now harvested by a very big and very expensive and very complex one called a combine. The combine marches through the fields, picking and husking the corn in one step. The ears are then brought in from the field and tossed into a large steel bin with holes in the floor. Hot, dry air is forced up through the holes to dry the kernels artificially so the farmer won't have to wait a month for them to dry naturally. The ears are then placed on a conveyor belt and carried to the scalper.

The scalper strips the kernels from the cobs and the whole mess is poured onto screens that separate the cobs from the kernels. The kernels are poured into a gravity separator, to weed out the bad ones. The good kernels are cleaned and polished with metal brushes. After that, they're fumigated to kill bugs, packaged, and sent to market.

Remember all that time, money, sweat and machinery the next time you unconsciously munch through a bag of popcorn.

The War Against Popcorn

Something as friendly as popcorn ought not to have enemies. But it does and they have legs and mean names like seed corn beetle, seed corn maggot, wireworm, white grub, corn root aphid, corn borer, earworm and chinch bug. Most of these insects lurk in the soil and attack the seed and roots, crippling the plants.

If the corn is strong enough to fight off the insects, it must next battle disease. Popcorn is basically a healthy plant, but in years when the temperature, moisture, or soil conditions are abnormal, popcorn can get sick. Corn diseases attack during the wet seasons when fungi and bacteria thrive. The brigade of diseases is just as gruesome as the brigade of insects: diplodia, gibberella, anthracmose, seed rot, stalk rot, root rot, ear and kernel rot, smut, leaf blight, bacterial wilt, rust and crazy top.

Now comes the last of popcorn's dreaded enemies:

Rats and mice.

Farmers try to hide the corn in steel bins, but even steel isn't foolproof. These little devils can squeeze through holes the size of a quarter to eat all they can get their wicked little teeth on. Rats can even chew through iron. The battle between farmers and rats and mice has been going on forever, and will probably go on forever. A rat, with a brain about the size of a sick grape, fools all the great corn-bin-building brains. It will be a great person who outthinks a rat and designs the completely rodent-proof grain bin.

Maybe that great person will be you.

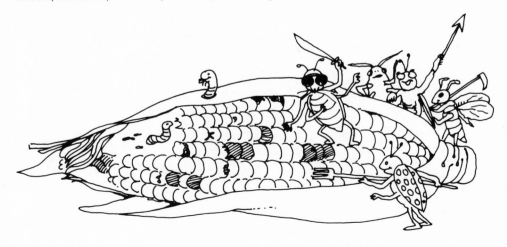

Growing Your Own Popcorn

Popcorn kernels are also popcorn seeds. In the old days, when you wanted to plant popcorn, you just stripped the kernels off last year's ears and stuck them in the ground.

That won't work anymore.

Man has tinkered with popcorn so much—through hybridization—that the kernels you grow in your garden aren't any good as seeds anymore. So every year, you have to buy brand new seeds.

Popcorn seeds can be hard to find. And if you do find them at the hardware store or supermarket, they might be too old. You'd be a lot better off to buy your seeds directly from a mail-order seed company. That way, you're sure to get the same high quality seeds the farmers plant.

Plant popcorn in the spring after the danger of frost has passed. A local gardener should know the best time to plant in your area.

Soak the seeds in water for twelve hours before planting. Plant them in clod-free soil that gets plenty of sun. Set them one to one and a-half inches deep, and about eight to ten inches apart. If you want to test your seed, sow one row, water every few days, and wait. If most of the corn is

POPCORN

9¢

POP

up and growing within one week, your seeds are good. Plant the rest of them. If two weeks pass with little or no growth, the seeds are bad.

Plant the seeds in blocks of short rows instead of one or two long rows. When planted in blocks, the plants will fertilize each other when the wind blows the pollen around. Blocks of plants can also support each other during high winds.

Keep the soil damp. If your popcorn seems to grow slower than your other corn, don't worry. Popcorn always grows slower than other corns. Just keep weeding the patch and be careful not to pull out the popcorn shoots.

When the stalks are knee-high, heap up soil around the exposed roots to give the plant extra support. When the tassels show, you know the ears are forming. Water deeply. Depending on where you live and what type of popcorn you're growing, the ears will be ready to pick within eighty-five to one hundred and twenty days.

Don't pick the ears until the stalks and husks are brown and the kernels are hard. If you can make a mark on a kernel with your thumbnail, the popcorn isn't dry enough to be picked. Let it hang a little longer.

Once you pick the ears, shuck off the husks and store the ears in an unheated, well ventilated outdoor building. Or chuck them into onion bags and hang them in a shed so the popcorn dries evenly.

After two or three weeks, strip the kernels off the ears by rubbing the ears together. If dry enough, the kernels should rub off easily. Put the kernels in an airtight container and freeze for five days to kill any insects. Take the popcorn out of the freezer, but keep it in the airtight container. On a windy day, pour the kernels from one bucket into another. The chaff and bee wings will blow away. You'll be left with pure, poppable popcorn.

If you grow popcorn during an extremely dry summer, your popcorn might get too dry. The wet weather in the fall will usually return moisture to the kernels. If your popcorn still pops small and you end up with a lot of old maids, you need to put moisture back into the popcorn. See the chapter "How to Put Life Back Into Old Maids."

Popcorn contains more food energy
than 96 percent of all edible foods.
(And 597 percent more food energy than beach sand)

Can Man Live on Popcorn Alone?

The rotten thing about snacks is that most of the time they aren't all that good for us.

They're expensive and loaded with empty calories and preservatives and sugar that attacks our teeth. And they ruin our appetite for the meal we're supposed to eat at home, and then whoever fixed the meal is hurt because we're not eating it.

Face it.

Snacks take all the fun out of snacking.

Hard-core snackers have one of two choices. We can stop snacking. Or we can snack on popcorn. Because popcorn is actually good for us.

Popcorn is low in fat and calories. Both can make us gain weight and increase our chances for heart disease. But when we eat popcorn, we're mostly eating air. So a whole gallon of unbuttered popcorn weighs only three and one-half ounces and has three hundred and ninety calories. A cup has only fifty-five calories.

Popcorn doesn't have any artificial coloring or preservatives. Doctors suspect that too much of some artificial colorings and preservatives can be bad for you.

Popcorn has no sugar. Sugar acts with bacteria in your saliva to decay your teeth. Doctors also worry that too much sugar can be bad for you in other ways. After sugar gives you a quick surge of energy, it may make you feel tired and depressed.

Popcorn has more nutrients than most other snacks. In fact, popcorn has more protein than any other corn or cereal grain, more iron than eggs, spinach, peanuts or roast beef, and more phosphorous and fiber than potato chips, ice cream cones, pretzels or saltine crackers.

Not bad for a snack.

Even the American Dental Association likes popcorn. Popcorn's dry, spongy texture helps clean the teeth and massage the gums—preventing gum diseases. The calcium in popcorn helps build teeth, too.

Whether you believe it or not, popcorn is disgustingly good for you. Someone figured out that if you ate nothing but popcorn and water, with a little help from cheese and beans, you could live comfortably without any other foods for a moderate length of time.

But before you give up other foods, think about this:

An average American man needs two thousand, nine hundred calories a day. One gallon of popcorn has only three hundred and ninety calories. To get all the calories he needs, a man would have to eat over seven gallons of popcorn each day.

Popcorniness

The Indians told stories to remember when to plant popcorn.

"If you live near apple trees," they said, "plant popcorn when the apple blossoms open."

"If you live near oak trees," others said, "plant when oak leaves are the size of a squirrel's ear."

When farmers were in the boast-

An old-fashioned husking bee.

banks were competing for attention. But they all looked just about alike, so it was hard to tell one from another. Except that one had a popcorn wagon set in front of it. The bank put the wagon on its stationery and checks. It eventually became known as the Popcorn Bank, and grew to be the most successful bank on the square.

Just after the turn of the century, popcorn was so popular that people wrote songs and poems about it. This put popcorn in a very special class. (How many songs have you heard about oysters?) To give you an idea of what they were like, here's one song and three poems. The poems were recipes that rhymed.

Best Evers

Four tablespoons of water boiled
   With sugar, just one cup;
Cook till its bubbles big declare
   That it is "waxing up";
When dropped in water cold it makes
   A soft and sticky ball,
Now crush some popped or buttered
   corn
   And slowly pour it all

Into the well-whipped white of egg,
   And stir it constantly;
Then spread on wafers of saltines

ing mood, they explained that they'd seen days so hot that popcorn kernels popped off the ears while they were still growing.

Before farm machines, neighbors met in late October every year for corn husking bees. They sat in a big group and yakked while they husked the corn. Occasionally, there'd be a red ear among all the yellow ones. Whenever someone found a red ear, that person could kiss whomever he or she wanted. This was a chance too good to pass up. So some of the older kids smuggled in their own red ears and pretended to find them in the pile. They'd do more kissing than husking.

On a town square in the East, four

To brown in oven, you see.
They surely are delicious bits
    To eat with cream or ice!
The boys who "pop" and girls who
        "cook"
    Will find them always nice.

Buttered Popcorn

The buttered popcorn's simply made!
    Just turn into a large deep pan,
And place in the oven the popped
        corn
    To make it brittle as you can.

Then pour the melted butter o'er
    And stir the whole mass steadily
Sprinkling with salt that it may cling
    Before things cool down "to a T".

Hunky-Dories

First grate a cake of chocolate sweet
    Into a dish which stands
In pan of boiling water near.
    When melting, it demands

A spoonful of the best rich cream;
    Then quickly in it beat
Two cups of freshly popped white
        corn
    And cup of pecan meat.

Stir briskly with a fork until
    The syrup covers all;
Dip out on sheets of paper waxed,
    And dry the nuggets small.

A Song of Popcorn

Sing a song of popcorn
    When the snowstorms rage;
Fifty little brown men
    Put into a cage.
Shake them till they laugh and leap,
    Crowding to the top;
Watch them burst their little coats
    Pop! Pop! Pop!

Sing a song of popcorn
    In the firelight:
Fifty little fairies
    Robed in fleecy white.
Through the shining wires see
    How they skip and prance
To the music of the flames:
    Dance, dance, dance.

Sing a song of popcorn—
    Done the frolicking:
Fifty little fairies
    Strung upon a string
Cool and happy, hand in hand
    Sugar-spangled, fair:
Isn't that a necklace fit
    For any child to wear?

59

Popping Enough Popcorn to Cover the United States

(Facts you'll never have to know)

- On the average, popped popcorn takes up to thirty-seven times as much room as unpopped popcorn. If you had enough unpopped kernels to cover the state of Wyoming, and then popped them, you could cover the United States with popcorn. Check the rooms in your house. Find one about ten feet wide, fourteen feet long, and eight feet high. If you poured a layer of popcorn kernels about two and one half inches deep on the floor and then popped them, the room would fill up. (You'd need about one inch of oil)

- Americans eat more popcorn than anyone else. The biggest popcorn eaters live in the Midwest—Kansas, Nebraska, Minnesota, the Dakotas, Indiana, Illinois—where most popcorn is grown. Minneapolis/St. Paul is the popcorn-eating capital of the world. The people there eat about four pounds a year apiece. New Yorkers eat less popcorn than anyone in America. Europeans don't seem to like it, but the Chinese love it

- Most popcorn is grown in the United States, but some is grown in South Africa, Hungary, Spain, Greece, Yugoslavia, France, Italy, Israel, Australia, China and most South American countries.

- The favorite seasons for eating popcorn are the fall and winter, with summer far behind.

- Believe it or not, there is actually a National Popcorn Week. It's the week before Halloween. That's the time when popcorn is traditionally harvested.

- The 5,600-year-old popcorn ears found in the Bat Caves of New Mexico ranged from smaller than a penny to two inches. Today, some ears of popcorn measure up to one and one-half feet long. Most are about six inches long.

- To dial time in San Francisco, dial P-O-P-C-O-R-N.

- The size of an average uncooked popcorn kernel is one-half inch long and one-eighth inch wide. It weighs more before it's popped because water escapes when it's popped.

- The "Billion Dollar Baby" is the largest reported kernel ever popped. With a circumference of thirty-seven centimeters, the Billion Dollar Baby weighs in at .0031 karats.

- In 1924, Cloid H. Smith was concerned because the popcorn sold in his cardboard cartons was drying out. He took his problem to the American Can Company. An engineer there developed the first air-tight metal can. That can was the forerunner of today's beer and pop cans.

Billion Dollar Baby

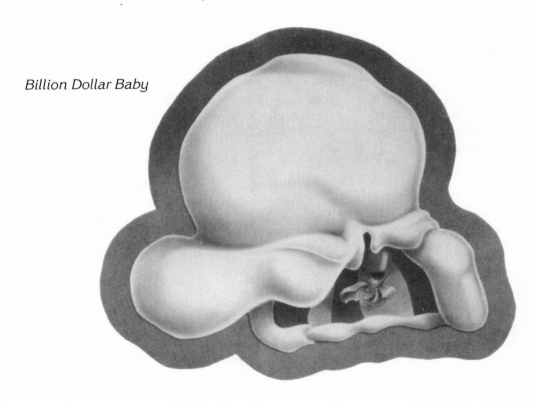

The evolution of Jolly Time Pop Corn from cardboard carton to can.

- The American Pop Corn Company sponsored a weekly radio show in the 1930s. The orchestra, called "General Jolly Time and his Popcorn Kernels," presented the music. Their most popular song was "A Bowl of Popcorn, a Radio, and You."

- The largest popcorn cribs in the world are in Sioux City, Iowa. Each crib is two and one-half stories high, a city block long, and holds four million pounds of popcorn.

What to Do With Popcorn
Besides Eating It

- Catch mice with it. They love popcorn. That's why they're such a big problem to popcorn growers. Just put a kernel, popped or unpopped, in a mouse trap. If you have a mouse in the house, you won't for long.

- Feed it to a cow. Farmers do. When popcorn kernels are damaged by frost or rats or whatever, farmers will grind it up and feed it to their cattle. Don't offer it to hogs, though. They don't like it.

- Feed it to pigeons. Many pigeon raisers feed popcorn to their pigeons because it's so good for them.

- Toss unpopped popcorn into the water to attract fish while you're fishing. It puts them in the mood to bite.

- Make popcorn bread. In 1946, there was a wheat shortage. President Truman let bakers use only three-quarters of the wheat flour they normally used. So one large bakery in Chicago decided to replace the missing wheat with popcorn flour. The bakery called their bread the "Popcorn Bread Syndicate." It cost fifteen cents a loaf compared to normal thirteen cents for an all-wheat loaf. The bakery also made popcorn muffins and popcorn doughnuts.

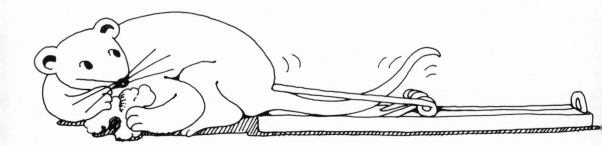

Popcorn bread is now making a comeback. Some bakers have recently put sawdust in bread to increase the fiber content. The United States government decided sawdust isn't healthy and banned it. Some bakers are now putting ground-up popped popcorn in their bread to provide fiber.

- Send gifts in it. During World War II, one man reported seeing ammunition packed in popcorn to cushion the shocks of the long ocean voyage. In 1951, one company shipped bottles of pills in popcorn. The company conducted an experiment to prove popcorn's shock resistance. A glass jar packed in ten ounces of popcorn was dropped sixty feet from the top of the building. Another glass jar was packed in twenty-four ounces of shredded paper and dropped. The glass packed in popcorn was unharmed, while the glass jar packed in shredded paper shattered.

The government wasn't wild about companies using popcorn as a packing material. They knew the popcorn would become contaminated when it was shipped and they were afraid someone would eat it and get sick. They were also afraid dishonest people would try to sell it after it was contaminated. So the government said that all popcorn used for packing must be dyed a repulsive color to prevent anyone from eating it. Since new plastic packaging materials have been developed, popcorn is rarely used.

Pop Arts and Crafts

All your life, people have nagged you, "Don't play with your food." And all your life, you've resented them.

Well, here's your chance to play with your food with no nagging. Maybe those naggers will even join you.

- Try stringing popcorn on red and green cord with cranberries to decorate a Christmas tree. (Someone is now making strings of plastic popcorn so you can use it year after year. Swell.)

64

- A few years back, there was a Pop Art contest. People strung popcorn on wire thread to make flowers, wreaths, even basketballs. Try it yourself. You never know when you'll need a popcorn basketball.

- It's easy to make popcorn sculpture. First, follow this recipe for a small batch:

Two quarts popped popcorn
One cup sugar
One-third cup light corn syrup
One-half cup water
Food coloring—if you want different colors of popcorn
(If you want more, double, triple or quadruple this recipe)

Pop your popcorn, put it in a buttered baking pan, and warm it in an oven that's been heated to about 250°F. While the popcorn is warming, mix the sugar, corn syrup, and water together. Put the syrupy mix in a pan and set the pan over a medium heat burner. Stir it constantly until the syrupy mix measures 265°F on a candy thermometer. Take it off the heat and add the food coloring. Now take the warm popcorn out of the oven and pour the syrupy mix over the popcorn. Stir the whole batch with a large spoon until the syrupy mix is evenly distributed over the popcorn.

Now you're ready to mold the popcorn into the shapes you want. If you mold the popcorn with your hands, wear rubber gloves to keep the popcorn from sticking to you. You can also make molds with wax paper or styrofoam cups. You'll have to work quickly before the mixture gets cold and hard to handle. Use toothpicks to fasten one shape to another, or to fasten eyes and noses and hats. Use pipe cleaners for arms or legs or whiskers. Use other foods and materials for decorations. For example, use gumdrops or raisins or scraps of cloth for eyes and noses.

Popcorn sculpture can be small. You can make little figures or people or animals or snowmen or houses or whatever.

Popcorn sculpture can also be big. Some have been as tall as twenty feet, weighing over one thousand pounds. The World's Largest Popcorn Ball weighed four hundred and fifty pounds and was four feet, five inches tall. In it were one hundred and sixty-four pounds of popcorn, one hundred and fifty pounds of sugar, eight gallons of syrup, and eight gallons of water.

- You can also make popcorn pictures. Paste the popcorn to heavy construction paper. Use plain popcorn for clouds or snow. Use food coloring on the popcorn for flags and cars.

Popcorn Recipes

There's a group of people out there somewhere, and I don't know who they are, who spend their lives testing and writing recipes. We owe them a lot. They make all our mistakes for us. And they are very courageous. Think of all the failures they have to eat.

Everybody has different ideas of how good food tastes. Even the recipe makers. So some of the recipes we see seem awfully good, while others seem just awful. (For instance, colonial housewives poured milk over popcorn and ate it like cereal.) Here are a few of the popcorn recipes I've found. It's up to you to decide which are good and which aren't.

POPCORN MEAT LOAF

1½ lbs. ground beef

1 cup ground popcorn

1 beaten egg

1 teaspoon Worcestershire sauce

1 small onion, chopped

Combine all the ingredients. Bake in a moderate oven for one hour. Serve with tomato sauce. Makes good hamburgers, too.

CHOCOLATE CHIP CORN

3 quarts popped corn

1½ cups granulated sugar

1½ tablespoons butter

1 square unsweetened chocolate

Boil the granulated sugar, butter, chocolate and three tablespoons of water to 242°F. Pour it, while hot, over the popped corn. Stir until all the kernels are coated. Let it cool on waxed paper.

POPCORN SOUP

1 quart milk

1 can of regular corn

Cracker crumbs

Dash salt, pepper

Tablespoon butter

Handful popcorn

Scald milk along with one can of corn. Press through a sieve and add salt, pepper and butter. Thicken with crackers and popcorn.

POPCORN, PEANUT BUTTER AND JELLY SANDWICHES

2 quarts popped corn

Peanut butter

Cherry Jelly

Corn Syrup

Drizzle hot syrup over corn, and stir until uniformly coated. Press a thin layer of popcorn into well-greased jelly-roll pan. Allow to cool. Cut into squares and spread half the slices with peanut butter and jelly. Top with a second slice.

POPCORN BALLS

2 cups granulated sugar
1 cup light corn syrup
1 cup water
3 tablespoons butter

Combine ingredients and cook to 260°F. Pour over two quarts salted popcorn. Mix thoroughly and mold into balls. Be careful not to burn hands with hot syrup. Let cool on waxed paper.

POPCORN CEREAL

Pop the popcorn and serve with cream & sugar.

VACATION ISLAND CRUNCH

8 cups salted popcorn
1 cup salted pecans
2 12-oz. cans root beer

1 cup sugar
½ cup light corn syrup
½ cup butter or margarine
¼ teaspoon salt

Combine popcorn and pecans in a buttered bowl. Pour root beer slowly down side of heavy saucepan; add sugar, syrup, butter and salt; stir gently but well. Bring to a boil, stirring until sugar melts. Cook to 290°F. Pour in a fine stream over popcorn and pecans; toss gently until popcorn is coated with syrup. Spread onto two buttered baking sheets and separate with a fork. Cool. Makes twelve cups.

CHILI CORN

4 quarts popped corn
3 small dried red chilies
1 package (6¾ oz) peanuts

1 package (3½ oz) roasted sunflower seeds
6 tablespoons soft margarine
¾ teaspoon garlic salt

Heat corn in oven if it's cold. Cook chilies and peanuts in margarine over low heat for 5 minutes. Remove chilies. Add sunflower seeds and pour over hot corn. Season with garlic salt.

CARAMEL CORN

1 cup sugar
½ cup corn syrup
2 tablespoons molasses
½ cup water

1 tablespoon butter
½ tablespoon vinegar
3 quarts popped popcorn

Combine all ingredients except popcorn. Cook until syrup becomes brittle when tested in cold water. Pour over popped corn, stirring while pouring. Let cool on buttered platter.

POPCORN CHOP SUEY

½ cup molasses
½ cup corn syrup
½ tablespoon butter

5 cups popped popcorn
½ cup grated coconut
½ cup shelled peanuts

Mix molasses and syrup with vinegar and boil slowly to prevent burning until a bit dropped in cold water will become brittle. Remove from fire, add butter and pour over popcorn. Mold balls as it cools.

Index

73